NOT ONE DROP

NOT ONE DROP

THE BIBLICAL END OF OUR WORLD

ELMER M. HAYGOOD

NOT ONE DROP
THE BIBLICAL END OF OUR WORLD

iUniverse books may be ordered through booksellers or by contacting:

iUniverse
1663 Liberty Drive
Bloomington, IN 47403
www.iuniverse.com
1-800-Authors (1-800-288-4677)

Scripture references: Scofield Study Bible, 1976 Edition, Authorized King James version, Oxford Press

ISBN: 978-1-5320-0527-5 (sc)
ISBN: 978-1-5320-0526-8 (e)

Library of Congress Control Number: 2016913622

Print information available on the last page.

iUniverse rev. date: 08/22/2016

Preface

We live in a beautiful world with its various geographical regions. A few times as I stood on the beautiful beaches of Florida and looked out upon the Gulf of Mexico and the Atlantic Ocean, I wondered why there is so much water on the earth, especially water that is undrinkable. I believe in the biblical account of creation so I had to wonder why God created this world with so much water. I began to search through the Bible for scriptures and events that involved water. I became engrossed in a highly mentally stimulating excursion from Genesis to Revelation that revealed the physical and spiritual importance of the simple molecule of water. I am sharing my extensive research which I endeavored to make very clear for the average reader.

I am fascinated with the physical sciences and I am an advocate for the application of our current scientific knowledge into our biblical studies which helps us understand how certain events unfolded even though they were divinely inspired. An example of such an event is the transformation of Lot's wife to a pillar of salt in the book of Genesis. It was amazing to realize that one simple event was related through water to the end of the world.

In writing this book I face the prospect of criticism due to a lack of specific formal credentials or an extensive record of formal Bible studies. Many people without the credentials have the same desire to know and, since we are all God's children, He will not withhold insights into the scriptures because of credentials. This book is written with the freedom I have to ask, to seek answers and to formulate inspired understandings into writings. One goal of this book is to encourage the average Bible students to go beyond the weekly programmed studies and seek freely and confidently to understand things in the Bible that at first seem very complex and mysterious but really need further clarification. Their efforts might help others to get a better understanding of what the scriptures or the biblical events are really revealing to us. I hope this book helps the fire of curiosity burn brighter.

Introduction

I believe some of the mysteries surrounding the beginning and the ending of our world can be explained by the many details given by the scriptures and the application of the scientific knowledge we have acquired to date. Even though the beginning and the end initially result from divine actions, the events that followed those actions are definable by principles of science. The universe as we know it today is believed to be a product of a singular event called the Big Bang. The end of creation will also be a product of a singular event that will cause the total destruction of the current heaven and earth. This singular event will be the precursor to the ushering in of a new earth and the new heaven.

I view the creation as an intelligently planned work of art and it reflects the creative processes of a divine artist. A painter or sculptor who plans a project sets out the materials that are needed to create the project and the materials that are chosen define the artist. A sculptor or painter is not just a painter or sculptor but a sculptor of wood, or metal or ice, or a painter of a certain style. The artist might combine many materials but there is normally a primary material or style that he is known by and that material or style can be found in all his works. Once the artist begins to create, he continues with the chosen materials until his vision is completed. The Creation also occurred in such an artistic manner. God prepared his materials and used a workstation that comprised the vastness of space. A principal element dominates creation and that element is "water". Water is the primary element in the total accumulation of materials that comprise what is called in the Bible as "the deep". Some people might believe the deep was approximately the size of Earth; however, I believe it was large enough to contain all the materials for the formation of the entire universe. Everything gigantic or minute, organic or inorganic in the universe originated from the water and the elements in the deep.

The book of Genesis says that God created the heaven and the earth and it enumerates the many facets of creation that were completed during the six days of work. Four of the six days involved the manipulation of water in various stages and the appearance of things out of water. But, for the end of the heaven and the earth there are no detailed descriptions of what will initiate the destruction of the earth and the heaven even though there are many scriptures that describe an earth and heaven in great peril. The accounts of the destruction as given in the scriptures make one believe that the heavens, the earth and the solar system will be destroyed by an unleashing of a great fire from God. This book will show that an unleashed blanket of fire upon the earth will not be necessary. God will act in one very specific manner as he has throughout the Bible and this one discriminate act will lead to the utter destruction of the earth and our solar system. God will manipulate the simple molecules of water as he has done historically to accomplish great biblical events. The same manipulation of water will be the manner by which the heavens and the earth will be destroyed.

There are some crucial facts about the Bible that must be kept in mind as you read this book:

1. The Bible was written many years ago for all men past and present.
2. When men in the Bible were inspired to write their visions of the future they were not given an upgraded vocabularies or an understanding of future advancements in scientific knowledge.
3. Biblical writings were done in the vocabulary and understanding of the time period in which the writers lived.
4. We have to apply our current knowledge to the biblical visions in order to get a better understanding of what was recorded.

The Bible is a complicated composite of history, laws, and spiritual teachings and prophesies which requires that we apply the full weigh of our knowledge to it. When we do, we will discover some highly interesting and perhaps unknown facts such as the critical relationship of water to the beginning and ending of our world.

Chapter 1 – How Our World Was Formed

In order to get a better understanding of how the world will end we need to take a closer look at its beginning. Scientists look towards the universe for the origin of the earth but I believe they should look to Earth for the origin of the universe.

> *Genesis 1: 1-3- In the beginning God created the heaven and the earth. And the earth was without form, and void; and darkness was upon the face of the deep. And the Spirit of God moved upon the face of the waters. And God said, Let there be light: and there was light.*

I believe the scriptural reference to the deep is not a reference to water as simple H2O. The deep was a grand concoction of elements laid out by God in preparation for the six days of creation work. To this concoction was applied compression which produced the celestial bodies of the universe, the earth and its solar system. The Spirit of God applied a swaddling web of uniform pressure to the massive quantity of material in the deep. The pressure produced an astronomical degree of heat within the deep and a multitude of thermal reactions on a grand scale. The continuous pressure and heat caused the formation of an abundance of elements and masses of all sizes and configurations within the deep. The interior became as an uncovered bowl of oatmeal and water boiling in a microwave oven. The compression and heat resulted in a violent explosion and a gargantuan splatter against the walls of God's workstation of space. I believe this gargantuan splatter was what is commonly referred to as the Big Bang. The universe was formed with its diverse patterns of galaxies, stars, comets and other celestial bodies (See Compression Factor Diagram). It was not necessary for God to create stars and other celestial bodies individually because the single act of uniform compression resulting in the Big Bang created all in a more logical and efficient manner.

Scientists are diligently searching for the presence of water in the universe in order to determine the origin of life on Earth. In view of the compression factor, the masses that burst forth from the deep carried water outward into space. However, the only celestial bodies that will be found with water or ice are those without a persistent molten core. These traveled into deep space, rapidly cooled, and preserved water or ice in their interiors or on their surfaces. For instance, a small mass like a comet that ejected from the deep without a heated core could potentially have a presence of water or ice if it left the deep with water embedded in its composition.

> COLLEGE PARK, Md. -- Scientists for <u>Deep Impact</u>, the University of Maryland-led NASA mission that made history when it smashed into a comet this past July 4th, have added another first to their growing

list: the first finding of water ice on the
surface of a comet.
(University of Maryland, UM News Desk,
February 5, 2013)
(http://www.newsdesk.umd.edu/scitech/
release.cfm?ArticleID=1213ds)

Some larger masses without molten cores also traveled
like hot coals from a recently extinguished campfire. They
traveled with steamy surfaces that also cooled rapidly as
they reach the cold outer space. The rapidly cooling steam
embedded water or ice into their surfaces.

After the background of stars and other celestial
bodies were spread upon the canvas of space, the web of
divine pressure continued to tighten towards the center of
compression. The remaining materials were locked in not
free to splatter outward. They were as the remaining water
and oatmeal in the microwave after a large portion of the
mixture has splattered against the sides. The remaining
water and other elements were prepared for the formation
of our solar system, the unformed and void earth and its sun.

In a large portion of the water of the unformed earth,
God split the water molecules and allowed the hydrogen
atoms to rise far beyond the area of the earth. Once the
hydrogen reached the desired height, the Spirit of God
compressed it to make the ever exploding hydrogen sun.
The compression of the singular hydrogen elements in the
absence of a massive coolant like water produced the ever
exploding phenomena of the sun.

> The Sun is, at present, about 70% <u>hydrogen</u> and 28% <u>helium</u> by mass everything else ("<u>metals</u>") amounts to less than 2%. (http://www.nineplanets.org/sol.html, January 25, 2009)

The process of collecting hydrogen from water is one that mankind is currently predicting to be the affordable fuel energy production of the future.

> Producing hydrogen from water may be achieved in several different ways such as electrolysis, direct solar, thermo-nuclear high temperature cracking, using catalysts, using biomaterials or using some form of chemicals to split water (H_2O) into H_2 (hydrogen) and O (oxygen). http://www.hydrogencarsnow.com/ hydrogen-from-water.htm (2016)

The Spirit of God demonstrated that the process worked well from the beginning of time as a reliable source of energy. The water molecules that were depleted of their hydrogen atoms for the formation of the sun became simple oxygen atoms. These oxygen atoms were lighter than the water molecules that remained in the deep and they separated to form the firmament. After the sun was created, the Spirit of God continued with a measured amount of uniform compression to the remaining water and material of the deep, or the unformed earth. The pressure continued to heat the interior which caused a heavy cloud of evaporation to cover the circumference of the unformed earth. The heavy overcast separated from the remaining water and a cloudy atmosphere developed.

> *Genesis 1:6-7 – And God said, Let there be a firmament in the midst of the waters, and let it divide the waters from the waters. And God made the firmament, and divided the waters which were under the firmament from the waters above the firmament and it was so.*

The continuous compression and tremendous heat also caused the elements in the water of the deep to coagulate into one mass. The massive coagulation was not allowed to burst forth like oatmeal in a microwave oven so; the mass began to rise from the water in volcanic fashion. It emerged as a hot steamy surface that eventually cooled in the firmament to become dry land. At the same time the water gathered together in a spherical shape due to the continuous uniform compression. The earth was formed with a singular massive land mass surrounded on all sides by water. The belief in a singular land surface as one supercontinent is a current theory of the formation of the earth before it divided into several continents. In the very beginnings of time Earth was called Pangaea.

> About 300 million years ago, Earth didn't have seven continents, but instead one massive supercontinent called Pangaea, which was surrounded by a single ocean called Panthalassa.

http://www.livescience.com/38218-facts-about-pangaea.html (December 17, 2014)

It must be noted that the dry land received a specific designation as "earth" and the water received a separate designation as "sea". We call the composite Earth but I believe the unique designation given to water implies that it has a distinct purpose in creation and it will be shown later in this book that it will have a distinct purpose at the end.

> *Genesis 1: 9-10 – And God said, Let the waters under the heaven be gathered together unto one place, and let dry land appear; and it was so. And God called the dry land Earth, and the gathering together he called Sea, and God saw that it was good.*
>
> *Genesis 2:6 –But there went up a mist from the earth, and watered the whole face of the ground.*

Then God created seeds in very fertile soil as a result of the volcanic process of land creation and the land and the seeds were watered by the mist evaporation from the land and the dispersion of volcanic steam.

The Compression Factor Diagrams

If a bowl of oatmeal and water is heated in a microwave oven, the heat in the center of the bowl will cause portions of the oatmeal to splatter throughout the inner chamber of the oven.

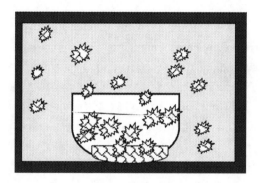

The immense heat created by the compression that was applied to the deep produced massive chemical reactions that spewed masses of various sizes and composition throughout the canvas of space.

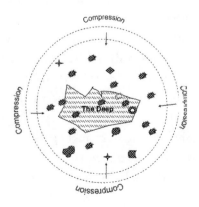

Chapter 2 – Water Balanced

The newly formed artwork of creation involving the earth covered by three-fourth water met God's plan for its existence and its future destruction. Astronomers tell us that our solar system consists of nine planets that revolve around the sun in fixed orbits. Each planet has successfully maintained its orbit for thousands or millions of years. In order for any object to remain in motion at the same rate and in the same pattern, there must be two stable factors: weight and force. In childhood we discovered that in order to keep objects turning around our heads on a string, a certain amount of force had to be applied and the weight of the objects determined how much force was needed. If the force is stable and the weight suddenly increases, then the object will begin to fall as it revolves around. More force would be needed. If the force is stable and the weight of the object is suddenly decreased, the force will cause the object to accelerate and possibly fly off the string into the distance. The planets also maintain their fixed orbits because of their stable weights and the stable force God has applied to them. They maintain their proper places like balls on a string. If either the weight or the force changes drastically, the pattern of revolution around the sun will also change. Such change would jeopardize the stability of the solar system.

Scientists say no verifiably significant amount of water or ice has been found on any planet in our solar system except Earth which is three-fourth water. Earth maintains its orbit around the sun because of the balance of the massive weight of water combined with the weight of dry land and the stable force that controls its orbit. The prophet Isaiah records in the Bible that God was mindful of the balance of the earth when it was formed. The earth is not a haphazard phenomenon but a well planned and deliberate project involving delicate measurements on a grand scale.

> *Isaiah 40:12 – Who hath measured the waters in the hollow of his hand, and meted out heaven with a span, and comprehended the dust of the earth in a measure, and weighted the mountains in scales, and the hills in a balance?*

If we believe that the Spirit of God created the heaven and the earth then we must believe as Isaiah says that the Spirit was mindful of the quantity and the importance of each facet of creation. There is a reason for the amount of water on the earth because the artist knows the purpose of his material and the message he wishes to convey. He also knows the most efficient way to undo what he has done. This book will show how God will manipulate water to destroy his heaven and earth.

Chapter 3 – Water as Earth's Coolant

As a product of compression, Earth was formed with a fiery center and the gathering together of the water formed a massive amount of coolant that limits the effects of the interior fires. The average person is not mindful of the fiery core because we are shielded in our daily life by the water and the earth's crust. We are made aware of the fire within during brief news broadcasts about a volcano eruption.

The molten core of the earth can reach a temperature of twelve thousand degrees Fahrenheit. The volcanic eruptions on the surface of the earth and under the great oceans are results of the tremendous heat generated at the core. The heat can be so intense that submarine volcanoes are pushed up from the bottom of the ocean in spite of the massive volume of water.

> New evidence deep beneath the Arctic ice suggests a series of underwater volcanoes have erupted in violent explosions in the past decade.

Jeanna Bryner, Live Science Managing Editor | June 27, 2008 01:05pm ET

> http://www.livescience.com/4992-volcanoes-erupt-beneath-arctic-ice.html

There are great fires beneath the surface and there is a great fire above the surface. Scientists report that the sun is a massive phenomenon of explosions that are equivalent to hydrogen bombs. The sun is ninety-three million miles from the earth yet it burns our skin, our land and raises the temperature of earth's massive waters. The surface temperature of earth is kept from the maximum possible due to the presence of water and its evaporative cooling properties.

In considering the fires within and the heat from the sun, I can say that without the presence of massive bodies of water, Earth would be as a small burning star whose fires would eventually consume its mass which means that the continuous existence of the physical earth is dependent upon the continuous presence of water. But, what if there is no water. The Bible gives us examples of such conditions and offers an understanding of the future prospect of the earth.

Chapter 4 – The Spirit of God Removes Water

God created the universe by calling out the "deep" which contained all the material for the making of the universe. The executor of the power of God that called out the deep is known in the Bible as the Holy Spirit. The Holy Spirit is often referred to in the Bible as "fire". It is crucial during Bible study to know the difference between a reference to natural fire and a reference to spiritual fire which is the Spirit of God. If the scriptures mention fire with reference to spiritual fire and the reader gives the connotation as natural fire, the reader then attributes to the spiritual fire all the properties of natural fire. The properties of natural fire and spiritual fire are worlds apart. Natural fire occurs within the realm of scientific principles and produces heat, smoke, odor and a residue as by-products of combustion. Spiritual fire works according to the will of God and does not conform to scientific principles thus, does not produce heat, smoke, odor or any by-products of combustion. An acknowledgement of the distinction between the two is imperative in understanding how the Spirit of God will cause the destruction of the heaven and the earth. There are four specific events in the Bible where the Spirit of God interacted specifically with water and these events guide us to an understanding of how the heaven and the earth will be on fire, dissolved and utterly destroyed. These four events are:

1. The Destruction of Sodom and Gomorrah
2. Elijah and the Prophets of Baal at Mt. Carmel
3. The Parting of the Red Sea
4. Elijah and Elisha at the Jordan River

The Destruction of Sodom and Gomorrah – Genesis Chapter 19

> *Genesis 19:26 – But his wife looked back from behind him, and she became a pillar of salt.*

The Bible states that Lot and his family were allowed to leave the doomed cities of Sodom and Gomorrah. Lot's wife looked back and was turned into a pillar of salt. I thought for many years that what happened to her was really strange and without a reasonable explanation. Why was she turned into a pillar of salt? Biologists tell us that the human body is over eighty percent water and the rest is a small variety of natural chemicals. If every molecule of water is removed from the body, only a small pile of chemicals would remain. These chemicals are mostly called salts and can be found in the nutrition facts of today's food containers, for example: niacin, calcium, thiamin, zinc, iron, phosphorous, magnesium, copper, sodium and others. All of these chemicals except copper and iron are described as a white crystalline substance with varying tints. I believe the appearance of the pillar of salt that represented Lot's wife was not like the refined salt that is used today for cooking but like natural salt that was just removed from the salt mines. Salt from the mines can have a yellowish and reddish tint which is an appearance with which the inhabitants of biblical times were familiar. The Spirit of God removed the water from Lot's wife which left a pile of natural chemicals. Lot's wife was returned to the state of man before God created him with the minerals of the ground, water and the breath of life. The remains of Lot's wife cannot be found because the pillar of salt that represented her was eroded to the ground by the wind so there was left no physical memorial of her. It became impossible to distinguish the minerals that belonged to her from the normal sand of the countryside. The demise of Lot's wife is an indication of the destruction that befell the cities of Sodom and Gomorrah.

It is recorded in Genesis 13:10 that Sodom and Gomorrah were well-watered and fertile and rivaled the Garden of Eden. The implication is that, after the wrath of God, the land was no longer well-watered or fertile.

> *Genesis13:10 – And Lot lifted up his eyes, and beheld all the plain of Jordan, that it was well watered everywhere, before the Lord destroyed Sodom and Gomorrah, even as the garden of the Lord, like the land of Egypt, as thou comest, unto Zoar*

In view of what happened to Lot's wife, I question a common belief that Sodom and Gomorrah were destroyed by a volcano. Can a volcano or natural fire destroy the land's access to water if it was originally well watered and fertile? The term "well watered" refers to an abundant and steady water supply. Can fire destroy the ability of the land to rebound with plant life after the fire has been extinguished? The following science report shows the long term beneficial effects volcanoes have on the land.

> While it is true that the immediate effect of volcanoes on plant life is death, the long term effect is very positive. Magma from the Earth's core contains a rich source of nutrients that plants need to survive. Each time a volcano erupts, it brings these nutrients with it. When volcanoes explode, spreading ash around a large area, this ash acts as a fertilizer, enriching the soil. It is no surprise that the soil near volcanoes is among the richest and most fertile on Earth. (http://www.kidsgeo.com/geology-for-kids/0052-volcanoes-and-plant-life.php)

If Sodom and Gomorrah was destroyed by a volcano the land would have rebounded and become potentially more fertile than before the destruction.

Some analysts believe that the cities were destroyed by an earthquake. The scriptures say that Lot was allowed to take his family to a small city in the plains called Zoar and Zoar would be spared. Lot took his two daughters from Zoar and they dwelled in a mountain.

> *Genesis 19:30 – And Lot went up out of Zoar and dwelt in the mountain and his two daughters with him; for he feared to dwell in*

> *Zoar: and he dwelt in a cave, he and his two*
> *daughters.*

Lot was afraid to reside in Zoar because the city was too close to Sodom and Gomorrah. Would it have been reasonable for the angels to permit Lot to reside in close proximity to the area of pending destruction if the manner of destruction was going to be an earthquake? Would it have been reasonable for Lot to be allowed to dwell in a mountain if there was going to be a massive earthquake that would swallow several cities? The angels demonstrated a desire to save Lot and his family. An earthquake also does not leave a land barren. The greatest catastrophe that renders a land completely barren is a sustained drought which is the absence of water. I believe the nature of the judgment against Sodom and Gomorrah and the other cities of the plain was the same that befell Lot's wife.

Genesis 19:24 says that God rained down fire and brimstone from heaven which might influence a reader to think of natural fire.

> *Genesis 19:24 – Then the Lord rained upon*
> *Sodom and upon Gomorrah brimstone*
> *and fire from the Lord out of heaven; And*
> *he overthrew those cities, and all the plain,*
> *and all the inhabitants of the cities, and that*
> *which grew upon the ground.*

An additional scripture that also makes the reader consider natural fire is Genesis 19:28 which states that

Abraham looked towards Sodom and Gomorrah early in the morning.

> *Genesis 19:27-28 – And Abraham got up early in the morning to the place where he stood before the Lord. And he looked toward Sodom and Gomorrah, and toward all the land of the plain, and beheld, and, lo, the smoke of the country went up as the smoke of a furnace.*

The report of fire and brimstone raining from heaven and smoke contribute to the idea of earthquakes and volcanoes. But, we have to consider other reports of the event such as can be found in the book of Lamentations.

> *Lamentations 4:6 – For the punishment of iniquity of the daughter of my people is greater than the punishment of the sin of Sodom that was overthrown as in a moment, with no hands stayed upon her.*

Lamentations indicates that the destruction of Sodom and Gomorrah occurred swiftly and there were no lingering events associated with it. A natural fire resulting from an earthquake or volcano that was great enough to totally destroy several cities beyond recognition would not have occurred swiftly. Also Abraham's actions as described in Genesis 19:27-28 gives an indication of the time of the event – Abraham observed the area early in the morning. His action also gives an understanding that the event was also not boisterous as an earthquake, volcano or a massive fire would be.

> *Genesis 19:27-28 – And Abraham got up early in the morning to the place where he stood before the Lord. And he looked toward Sodom and Gomorrah, and toward all the land of the plain, and beheld, and, lo, the smoke of the country went up as the smoke of a furnace.*

If Sodom and Gomorrah and all the plain were visible to Abraham, then Abraham was in close proximity to the areas of destruction. Abraham's night of sleep is not indicative of an earthquake or volcano in the region. How could he sleep through the night while the earth rumbled and as lava and fire spewed from a volcano in the area? There would have been widespread chaos in the cities and the adjoining regions and the event would have been recorded in the Bible. Abraham's night of sleep gives an idea of the mode of operation of the Spirit of God. The initial event occurred as quietly as the transformation of Lot's wife to a pillar of salt. In speaking of Lot's wife the scriptures give no indications of a rumbling of the ground, a roaring of thunder or a natural fire upon her body. There was only the transformation to salt. What transformed her to salt? Did the writer of the scripture omit the spiritual fire from God as is recorded in the book of Leviticus?

> *Leviticus 10:2, 5 – And there went out fire from the Lord, and devoured them, and they died before the Lord. (5) So, they went near,*

> *and carried them in their coats out of the*
> *camp, as Moses had said.*

In the above scripture the sons of Aaron were "devoured" in the sanctuary by fire from God yet they were carried out of the sanctuary in their coats. If the fire from God had performed with the properties of natural fire, the coats would have also been consumed, even first. If the fire from God "devoured" the men but did not devour their coats, it can be assumed that the compositions of the bodies were changed just like Lot's wife. The coats were sufficient to carry out their remains. If the Spirit of God demonstrated its power to eliminate Lot's wife from the earth by removing water which turned her into a pillar of salt, why would the same Spirit need to do anything different to the sons of Aaron and to the inhabitants of Sodom and Gomorrah? The Spirit of God, the fire and brimstone, transformed Lot's wife into a pillar of salt and the people, the animals and the plant life in the cities met the same fate. Not one drop of water was left from Lot's wife, the sons of Aaron or Sodom and Gomorrah.

If Sodom and Gomorrah was not destroyed by a natural fire, volcano or earthquake, there needs to be an explanation of Abraham's report of smoke as the smoke of a furnace.

> *Genesis 19:27-28 – And Abraham got up*
> *early in the morning to the place where he*
> *stood before the Lord. And he looked toward*
> *Sodom and Gomorrah, and toward all the*
> *land of the plain, and beheld, and, lo, the*

> *smoke of the country went up as the smoke of*
> *a furnace.*

So, what caused the image of smoke as viewed by Abraham? The destruction of the cities occurred in two phases.

> Phase 1 – The removal of water as exemplified in Lot's wife
> Phase 2 – The arrival of a fierce wind

After the Spirit removed the water from the people, the animals and the plants, they became pillars of salt scattered throughout the cities. The absence of water or moisture also caused the buildings, the wooden items and the clothes to become extremely fragile and crumble as though they were a thousand years old. Dried streams and the cities filled with pillars of salt and crumbling infrastructure marked the first phase of the destruction. An important point to remember is that men in the Bible described what they witnessed by using the best understanding and terminology of their time. Abraham was standing alone and was not being coached by the angels who had left the area. Abraham saw from a distance the common patterns of furnace smoke that consists of a narrow dark stream extending upward from the ground and spreading outward from the top. If Sodom and Gomorrah and the other cities of the plain were on fire at the same time, there would not have been any specific smoke patterns. Abraham's view of a localized dark stream rising from the ground can easily be compared to the weather pattern known as a tornado, whirlwind, or other such strong wind. I believe a strong wind was sent by God to gather up all the salt pillars and the remains of the infrastructure of the cities into a tremendous funnel cloud. Abraham was unable to discern the dynamics of such a wind from where he stood because the sound and the effects of the winds were basically localized and in short duration. Also, according to current weather reports in Israel, tornadoes are rare occurrences so, Abraham might not have had any experience or knowledge of such weather phenomenon.

> Israel experiences a tornado once in 15 years...
> http://www.israelweather.co.il/english/
> page2.asp?topic_id=70&topic2_id=146&
> sub_topic_id=1 (Tornadoes/Tornadoes in Israel)

There are no remnants of Sodom and Gomorrah and the other cities of the plain except sand and salt. I also believe that a definite product of the destruction of the cities is the extraordinary salinity of the Dead Sea. The remains of the cities were scattered across the plain and also deposited into the waters of the Dead Sea immediately and after periods of wind gusts and erosion.

> Other post-biblical names for the Dead Sea include the "Sea of Sodom," the "Sea of Lot," the "Sea of Asphalt" and the "Stinking Sea." In the Crusader period, it was sometimes called the "Devil's Sea."

All of these names reflect something of the nature of this lake.
(http://www.bibleplaces.com/deadsea.htm)
(Dead Sea/Names of the Sea)

The Dead Sea has some of the most saline water on earth; as much as 35% of the water is dissolved salts! That's almost six times as salty as the ocean! … What you'll see on the shores of the Sea is white, crystals of salt covering everything. And this is no ordinary table salt, either. The salts found in the Dead Sea are *mineral salts*, just like you find in the oceans of the world, only in extreme concentrations…
(http://www.extremescience.com/zoom/index.php/earth-records/37-dead-sea)
(Lowest Elevation: Dead Sea)

The destruction of Sodom and Gomorrah was a divine act of annihilation and the repentance by God for the existence of the totally immoral and unrepentant people. There was left not one drop of water in Sodom and Gomorrah. This book will show that the same fate awaits the whole earth which will be just as immoral and unrepentant in the future.

Elijah and the Prophets of Baal at Mt. Carmel – I Kings 18

I Kings 18:38 – Then the fire of the Lord fell, and consumed the burnt sacrifice, and the

wood, and the stones, and dust, and licked up
the water that was in the trench.

I Kings 18 relay the story of a spiritual duel between Elijah, a prophet of God, and the prophets of Baal, a false god. After the prophets of Baal had completed their ritual to their god and were unsuccessful in achieving a response, Elijah requested an altar to be built with a trench around it. Elijah prepared a sacrifice on the altar and had the sacrifice drenched with twelve barrels of water and the trench was filled with water. Elijah prayed and fire came down from God and consumed the water soaked sacrifice, the water soaked stones, the water soaked wood, the water soaked dust and removed the water from the trench. The fire at Mt. Carmel was the same fire that fell upon Sodom and Gomorrah and upon the sons of Aaron. It performed in the same manner by removing water from the sacrifice, the wood, and the stones and from the trench. All that pertained to the altar was turn to dust and the fire, the Spirit of God, consumed even the dust of the altar. It was total eradication.

The soaked sacrifice was transformed into a pile of chemicals; the stones and the wood became as if they were a thousand years old and crumbled like the buildings in Sodom and Gomorrah. A natural fire on an altar should not have crossed the water filled trench but the water was consumed as though a thirsty invisible animal gulped it. The resulting dry trench became like the streams and other bodies of water in Sodom and Gomorrah. The consumption of the dust refers to the fact that all the dust that pertained to the altar was removed or disposed of just as the pillars of salt from the inhabitants, plants and structures of Sodom and Gomorrah were. There was left nothing that pertained to the altar or the sacrifice.

Why did Elijah use water if he was expecting fire from God in the form of natural fire? A natural fire would have eventually destroyed the sacrifice and evaporated the water. But, Elijah knew he would see the swift action of the Spirit of God that would remove water in an instant and thereby destroy everything.

The Red Sea – Exodus 14 and 15, 29; Psalms 78 and 106; Isaiah 11, II Kings 2

The sea was replaced by dry land! How was that accomplished? There have been cinematic portrayals of God's deliverance of the Israelites from Pharaoh's army at the Red Sea. Were the cinematic portrayals correct or even possible? A closer look at the scriptures reveals again the interaction of the Spirit of God with water resulting in the removal of water, not the parting or the pushing aside of water.

> *Exodus 14:21 – And Moses stretched out his hand over the sea; and the Lord caused the sea to go back by a strong east wind all that night, and made the sea dry land, and the waters were divided.*

> *Exodus 14:29 – But the children of Israel walked on dry land in the midst of the sea;*

and the waters were a wall unto them on their right hand, and on their left.

Exodus 15:8 – And with a blast of his nostrils the waters were gathered together, the floods stood upright as a heap, and the depths were congealed in the heart of the sea.

Psalms 78:13 – He divided the sea, and caused them to pass through; and he made the waters to stand as an heap

Psalms 106:9 – He rebuked the Red Sea also, and it was dried up, so He led them through the depths as through the wilderness.

Isaiah 11:15 – And the Lord shall utterly destroy the tongue of the Egyptian Sea, and with his mighty wind shall he shake his hand over the river, and shall smite it in the seven streams, and make men go over dryshod.

There seems to be a common belief that the Red Sea was parted by a strong wind because Exodus 14:21 mentions a strong east wind. However, one scripture says that a strong east wind blew all night and parted the waters while other scriptures say that the waters were as a wall on the right and the left and, the sea was congealed or in a heap while the Israelites crossed. A fierce wind is not sufficient to part a pond and definitely not a sea. Water that is pushed outward in a man-made or natural enclosure will return to its starting point unless all of the water is pushed to another area of containment. Since the Bible states that the water of the Red Sea was a wall on both sides of the Israelite, that implies that a lot of water remained at the sides of the sea basin. The water maintained its position until the Israelites crossed the dry sea floor of the Red Sea. If a reader believes it really was a strong wind, then the reader must ask at what speed it blew. Was it like an EF-4 or EF-5 tornado with wind speed over 200 miles per hour? Is that enough wind strength to make a wedge in the sea? A tornado-like wind can leave a path of destruction on land but it is extremely difficult to understand how it can leave a path through water and also stack the water on the sides of the path. The wind phenomenon would have to be at least the width of the sea to affect the total width of the path at the same time and, it would have been necessary for the wind to blow incessantly. If a wind strong enough to part the sea blew constantly, how could the Israelites cross in such a wind? Also, if the wind parted the sea what brought enough water back to drown Pharaoh's army?

The Red Sea had existed for at least several thousands of years or more at the time of Israel's crossing. Most rivers become sustained waterways because they are constantly fed by connecting tributaries. Isaiah 11:15 indicates there were seven streams that fed the Red Sea. It was necessary to also dry the seven streams in order for the Israelites to cross on dry ground.

> *Isaiah 11:15 – And the Lord shall utterly destroy the tongue of the Egyptian Sea, and with his mighty wind shall he shake his hand*

> *over the river, and shall smite it in the seven*
> *streams, and make men go over dryshod.*

Rivers and streams that have existed for thousands of years can not be made dry by a wind blowing all night. If water is drained from a river or lake, it would take many days of searing sunshine to dry the thick mud and water pockets in the basin. The Israelites went over with their horses and wagons and chariots. So, how was the floor of a great sea made dry overnight and what is the puzzling phenomenon of the wind?

The Spirit of God removed a large portion of water from the width of the Red Sea and from its feeding tributaries. The water was removed from the areas as the water was removed from Lot's wife, Sodom and Gomorrah, the sacrifice and altar at Mt. Carmel and from the sons of Aaron. The Sprit of God showed its power to remove water at any time, in any place and at whatever magnitude or configuration it desired. The event occurred at the Red Sea in two phases as it did in Sodom and Gomorrah.

1. The Spirit removed water
2. God sends the wind

The Spirit of God removed water not only from the sea but also from the creatures, all the plant life and the debris that saturated the water and the sea floor. The sea had great depth which means there were extremely steep drops on both sides. Imagine the difficulty of entering an empty swimming pool with a depth of six feet from one end and exiting up the other end. Then imagine a depth of ten times or more that has to be entered and exited by women and children and horses and wagons. If God's only action was the removal of water from the sea, it would have been extremely difficult or even impossible for the people to navigate the distance to the sea floor, through the remains of plant life, marine life, boulders and other debris. So, the second phase involving the wind was then necessary. The wind that blew all night after the removal of water was like the wind in Sodom and Gomorrah. It pulverized the material that was in the sea basin and distributed it evenly along the sea floor to facilitate the passage of the people, the animals, the wagons and chariots. The wind performed as a natural rake or spreader. It is recorded in Psalms 106:9 that "He led them through the depths as through the wilderness" and the prophet Isaiah also records how God made the passageway manageable for the people to cross.

> *Psalms 106:9 – He rebuked the Red Sea also, and it was dried up, so He led them through the depths as through the wilderness.*

> *Isaiah 63: 13-14 – Who led them through the deep, like a horse in the wilderness, that they should not stumble? As a beast goeth down into the valley, the Spirit of the Lord caused him to rest; so didst thou lead thy people, to make thyself a glorious name.*

Isaiah says that God eased the movement along the steep drop to the sea floor at one end and the steep climb to the top at the other end. The people were able to enter the depths as a horse enters the valley and makes his way across to the other side and continues up out of the valley on a manageable incline without stumbling. This prepared passage was also accessible by Pharaoh and his army.

The cinematic portrayals of the Red Sea Crossing always show two tall walls of water in close proximity to the Israelites which caused them to cross in a slightly narrow corridor. After watching the scenes I often wondered why Pharaoh was foolish enough to lead his army through the same obviously miraculous passage. He would have surely recognized two walls of water as another plague from God and, after losing his son, would have hesitated, observed the phenomenon further and perhaps would have quit the chase. Then I realized the water trap God set for the Egyptians.

The Trap:
- The Israelites were told to camp by the sea as a trapped prey
- God removed the water from the sea but from a considerably much wider area than is shown in the movies
- The wind that blew all night conformed the sea bed to the terrain of the wilderness
- The Israelites began to cross as the pillar of cloud and of fire released the highly impatient Egyptians who were eager to continue their pursuit
- The Egyptians did not realize they were crossing a dry terrain that was once the sea floor because of what the wind had done and because the crossing occurred at dark. The crossing occurred in the early morning darkness according to Exodus 14:24.

> *Exodus 14:24 – And it came to pass that in the morning watch the Lord looked unto the host of the Egyptians through the pillar of fire and of the cloud, and troubled the host of the Egyptians…*

Definition of MORNING WATCH: the watch on a ship from 4 a.m. to 8 a.m.
www.merriam-webster.com/dictionary/morning%20watch

- Very early in the morning the Israelites began to cross and the Egyptians pursued them and drove into the prepared trap of the dry sea floor.
- God removed the wheels of the Egyptian chariots which hindered their chariots. He then replaced the water that drowned them.

The trap was perfect. The water did not flow back into the Red Sea basin but was replaced by the same Spirit that called out water as the deep during Creation and commanded it to gather unto one place. The same Spirit can separate molecules of water to form the sun or the atmosphere and, it can put atoms together to form molecules of water at whatever volume it desires. It can then make the water conform to whatever geometric pattern it pleases. The record of walls of water on either side of the Israelites as they crossed should not be a mystery to believers because we believe that God made the water to gather together in one place at Creation. If he can cause the quantity of water in the great oceans to gather unto one place, surely he can control the water of a sea.

The events of the Red Sea and Sodom and Gomorrah provide us an insight into God's pattern of manipulating water to achieve his will and this pattern will be evident on the day of the Lord when the heaven and the earth will pass away.

Elijah and Elisha at the Jordan River – II Kings 2:8, 14

> *II Kings 2:8, 14 – And Elijah took his mantle, and wrapped it together, and smote the waters, and they were divided hither and thither, so that they two went over on dry land. (14) And he took the mantle of Elijah that fell from him and smote the waters, and said, where is the Lord God of Elijah? And when he also had smitten the waters, they parted to the one side and to the other; and Elisha went over.*

What wind blew for Elijah and Elisha when they crossed the Jordan River on dry land? The Bible reports that the water parted after a strike from Elijah's mantle. Elijah and Elisha walked across the Jordan River on dry land without any accompanying natural phenomenon. The water parted to the sides just as the water of the Red Sea parted to the sides. Elijah and Elisha walked the full width of the Jordan River on dry land just as the Israelites walked the full width of the Red Sea on dry land. A part of the Jordan River was removed by the Spirit of God to allow two men to pass to meet the chariots of God. The Jordan River did not have nearly the depth of the Red Sea and did not need the wind to prepare the floor of the river for passage. The water was returned to its place after Elijah and Elisha crossed together. After Elijah was taken up the water was removed again for Elisha to cross alone. There was no accompanying wind at each crossing. There was only the Spirit of God. Those who believe that the wind parted the Red Sea must ask themselves whether the strike from Elijah's mantle was more powerful than or as powerful as the east wind.

The most vivid example of what God did at the Red Sea and at the Jordan River is recorded in the book of Joshua when the Israelites crossed the Jordan River on dry land in the presence of the Ark of the Covenant. The following scriptures highlight the removal of water, the termination of water from tributaries, and the return of the water to normalcy.

> *Joshua 3:15 – 16 – And, as they who bore the ark were come into the Jordan and the feet of the priests who bore the ark were dipped in the brim of the water (for the Jordan overfloweth all its bank all the time of the harvest) That the waters which came down from above stood and rose up in one heap very far from the city Adam, that is beside Zarethan; and those that came down toward the sea of the Arabah, even the Salt Sea, failed, and were cut off; and the people passed over right against Jericho.*

> *Joshua 4:18 – And it came to pass, when the priests who bore the ark of the covenant of the Lord, were come up out of the midst of the Jordan, and the soles of the priests feet were*

*lifted up unto the dry land, that the waters
of the Jordan returned unto their place, and
flowed over all its banks, as they did before.*

The four biblical accounts mentioned in this chapter outline the specific actions of the Spirit of God, the fire of God, in creating situations through the manipulation of water. An understanding of these accounts is crucial to understanding how the earth and the heaven will pass away.

Pillars of Salt

Lot's Wife

The Sons of Aaron

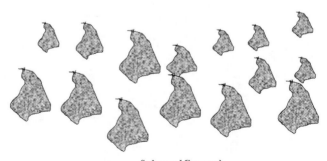

Sodom and Gomorrah

Red Sea Crossing

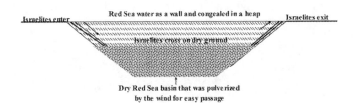

Red Sea water as a wall and congealed in a heap

Israelites enter

Israelites exit

Israelites cross on dry ground

Dry Red Sea basin that was pulverized
by the wind for easy passage

Jordan River Crossing

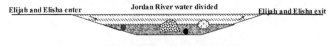

Jordan River water divided

Elijah and Elisha enter

Elijah and Elisha exit

Elijah and Elisha cross the dry Jordan River
basin that was untouched by the wind

Chapter 5 – A Deluge of Spiritual Fire Upon the Earth

The story of God's judgment against the cities of Sodom and Gomorrah in the book of Genesis is directly related to God's future judgment against the world in the book of Revelation.

> *Revelation 20:7- 9 – And when the thousand years are ended, Satan shall be loosed out of his prison, And shall go out to deceive the nations which are in the four quarters of the earth, Gog and Magog, to gather them together to battle; the number of whom is as the sand of the sea. And they went up on the breadth of the earth, and compassed the camp of the saints about, and the beloved city; and fire came down from God out of heaven, and devoured them.*

> *Revelation 21:1 – And I saw a new heaven and a new earth; for the first heaven and the first earth were passed away, and there was no more sea.*

What will happen between Revelation 20:9 and Revelation 21:1? The scriptures report a preparation for battle, fire from heaven and the coming of a new heaven and a new earth. The scriptures seem to show that the first heaven and the first earth will be disposed of by an undisclosed event. It seems that whatever will happen will involve the fire that will come down from God to destroy those who will amass to do battle with his saints. I believe the outpouring of fire in Revelation is a repeat of what happened at Sodom and Gomorrah when God rained down fire and brimstone to destroy the wicked cities. It is also similar to the fire that came down on Mt. Carmel for Elijah that destroyed the sacrifice and lapped up the water in the trench. The fire that destroyed Sodom and Gomorrah was focused in that particular area because that is where sin had festered and evoked the wrath of God. Revelation 20:8 states that the number of future combatants against God will be as the sand of the sea and from the four quarters of the earth. That is an indication that the fire that will come from God will be far reaching across the earth and will smite a great multitude of men, animals, plants, and also the great waters and streams. The result will be that most of the earth will become as barren as was Sodom and Gomorrah after the fire fell. The prophet Isaiah highlights the future plight of barrenness on the earth.

> *Isaiah 51:6 – Lift up your eyes to the heavens, and look upon the earth beneath; for the heavens shall vanish away with the smoke, and the earth shall wax old like a garment, and they that dwell therein shall die in like*

> *manner; but my salvation shall be forever,*
> *and my righteousness shall not be abolished.*

The fire that will fall from God will remove the water from the combatants who will have gathered to make war with him. The combatants, the waters and all the surroundings will be transformed from thriving to basic chemicals just as the inhabitants and infrastructure of Sodom and Gomorrah were transformed. They will appear to "wax old like a garment" that is depleted of every molecule of water. The great bodies of water will also be depleted of water just as the streams of Sodom and Gomorrah and the altar at Mt. Carmel. The water will be removed as the water was removed at the Red Sea and the Jordan River but will not be replaced. There will be no need to replace the water because when the fire falls in Revelation it will be the decisive action of God to destroy the world and all that dwell in it.

Those who did not gather to war against God will face the cataclysmic effects of the lost of the great waters on Earth. They will be in a state of utter hysteria as the earth quakes and causes the mountains and islands to collide. Chapter 2 of this book titled "Water Balanced" highlights the cooling effect of water and its role in the stability of the earth's orbit around the sun. What will be the result of a rain of fire from God so great that it annihilates most of the world's population and dries many streams and the great bodies of water? The aftermath will be the conditions that are described in the following scriptures: Isaiah 24:17-23, Isaiah 51:6, Jeremiah 24:17-23, Joel 2:1-2, 10, Joel 2:30-32,

2 Peter 3:7, 10-13, Psalms 114, Nahum 1:4-5, and Revelation 6:12-17.

The absence of the great waters will cause the earth to be like a deflated ball on a string that will begin to wobble in a decaying orbit around the sun.

> *Isaiah 24:17-23 – Fear, and the pit, and the snare, is upon thee, oh inhabitants of the earth. And it shall come to pass, that he who fleeth from the noise of the fear shall fall into the pit, and he that cometh up out of the midst of the pit shall be taken in the snare, for the windows from on high are open, and the foundation of the earth do shake, the earth is utterly broken down, the earth is clean dissolved, the earth is moved exceedingly. The earth shall reel to and fro like a drunkard, and shall be removed like a cottage; and the transgression thereof shall be heavy upon it, and it shall fall and not rise again.*

As Isaiah states, the earth will move forward and backward (to and fro) like a drunk man. This awkward movement will break up the mountains and the hills and send them tumbling across the earth as David reports in Psalms 114 where he says they will skip like rams and lambs:

> *Psalms 114:4 – The mountains skipped like rams, and the little hills like lambs.*

In conjunction with the violent land movements, the earth will also embark on an erratic and greatly accelerated orbit around the sun. It will be as a deflated ball that has flung free of the string. Without its water the earth will travel at an extremely accelerated rate because the weight has changed but the force or the gravitational pull of the sun is the same and, that force will increase as the earth continues to dissolve.

Isaiah also states that "the earth shall be removed out of its place" and "the earth is moved exceedingly" and, the earth "shall be removed like a cottage". The wobbling and the rapid acceleration will gradually tear the earth apart. Earth's appearance in space will be as a house that is gradually ripped apart as it is forced to move across the countryside as in the old days. The house gradually deteriorates and leaves a trailing path of debris behind it. The trail of debris will include large portions of the surface of the earth that will separate and expose the molten core. The appearance will support Isaiah statement that "the earth is utterly broken down, the earth is clean dissolved.

Accompanying the disintegrating earth in an erratic and accelerated pattern will be its moon. When the wrath of God is poured out as spiritual fire and smites water, the dry earth will be consumed with natural fire and smoke that will emanate from its unrestrained fiery core. The unrestrained fire will produce a global inferno as the gorges that were once great bodies of water become great fiery pits. One of the most commonly accepted mysteries of the calamity during the day of the Lord is the statements that the moon will be like blood and the moon will turn into blood as recorded in the books of Joel and Revelation:

> *Joel 2:30-31 – And I will show wonders in the heavens and in the earth; blood and fire, and pillars of smoke, the sun shall be turned into darkness, and the moon into blood, before the great and the terrible day of the Lord come.*

> *Revelation 6:12-17 – And I beheld, when he had opened the sixth seal, lo there was a great earthquake, and the sun became black as sackcloth of hair, and the moon became like blood…*

The descriptions in Joel and Revelation are examples of the attempts of the writers to give accurate reports of what they saw in their visions by using the limited understanding and terminology of their times. Their reports seem to imply that there will be a miraculous transformation of the moon into actual blood. The phenomenon of the moon's appearance as blood is not a mystery when the focus is on water. Moon explorations have revealed that the moon is barren and consist primarily of sand.

> Since there's nothing living on the moon, the soil is not a true soil like we're used to here. It's gray with very fine grained particles like sand or even dust and extremely dry because there is no water on the moon.

> (http://www.extremescience.com/zoom/
> index.php/space/35-space-science/77-
> about-the-moon) (Full Story on the Moon)

A fiery, fragmented and lighter earth that will be drawn closer to the moon of sand will cause the sand to ignite and liquefy. Sand will turn to glass at an extremely high temperature which is a common experiment in high school chemistry classes.

> Believe it or not, glass is made from liquid sand. You can make glass by heating ordinary sand (which is mostly made of silicon dioxide) until it melts and turns into a liquid. You won't find that happening on your local beach: sand melts at the incredibly high temperature of 1700°C (3090°F) (http://www.explainthatstuff.com/glass.html) (Glass)

Once the inferno of the earth ignites the surface of the moon and the surface liquefies, the moon will turn red from the heat and appear to be like blood. It is possible that large red molten masses of the surface will separate like great drops of blood. Revelation states the moon will be "like blood" which is possibly the initial phase of the surface thermal reaction and Joel states the moon will turn "into blood" which possibly describes a more advanced stage of liquefaction involving the separation of red molten masses from the surface. The moon whose gravitational force causes the formation of waves in the oceans of the earth today will have enough power to draw the weaken earth to it as they become a fiery duo in space.

> *Isaiah 24:19-20 –The earth is utterly broken down, the earth is clean dissolved, the earth is moved exceedingly. The earth shall reel to and fro like a drunkard, and shall be removed like a cottage; and the transgression thereof shall be heavy upon it, and it shall fall and not rise again.*

Utterly broken down! Clean dissolved! What do those terms really mean? I believe they mean that every stone from every mountain, hill and canyon across this planet will be broken and separated from the earth. Also, every stone of every mountain at the depths of the oceans will also be broken and separated from the earth. Every tree great or small across the world will be uprooted and set free from the foundation of the earth. Every stone and grain of dirt from all levels of the earth's crust plus the surface sand from the great deserts of the world, which has not been totally consumed by fire, will be peeled away and airborne. This also means that every structure and their contents across the world that sat on the dirt will be shattered and detached from the foundation of the earth. Every street or pavement or bridge of any kind across the world will be broken up into free flying chunks of asphalt and concrete. And, Also, I can imagine that every item of technology in utilities, communications, land, sea and air transportation, construction and warfare will be loose and airborne as they lose their connection to the earth. Utterly broken down and clean dissolved mean that the earth will be stripped down to its iron core.

As I was riding down a busy urban street I began to realize even more the full extent of those words. I saw flag poles, towers, fences, street signs, billboards, mailboxes, sewer covers, stoplights, trash cans and dumpsters, trailers and guard rails. All of these and other such items across the world will be free in space. I thought about Busch Gardens, an amusement park in my city, and then thought how all the great wheels, coasters and other entertainment structures, monuments and statues from across the world will also be in free orbits. When I arrived home I looked around and realized even further the full extent of "utterly broken down" and "dissolved". I saw washer and dryer, oven, refrigerator, water heater, air conditioning units, knives, forks, spoons, pots and pans, televisions, computers, printers, music systems, toilets, sinks, bathtubs, in-door and outdoors furniture and barbecue grills. I considered all of these from across the world and understood that space will be littered with giant heaps of trash from earth that will be like traveling landfills millions of miles long.

The Biblical visions are about the future but I wondered what it would be like if the earth dissolved today. I thought of the following which is an incomplete list of some of the highly explosive items of the world that would also be among the waves of debris and would be individually snared by the great pull of the sun. These items and those previously mentioned would be ablaze from the fires from the earth's core as they initiate individual orbits with trajectories that will eventually lead them to the sun.

- 17,000 nuclear warheads and 436 nuclear reactors
- Billions of cars and trucks with fuel
- Over 55,000 merchant ships plus the world's naval ships, cruise ships, yachts and personal and scientific vessels with fuel
- Over 15,000 trains with 20 to 300 or more cars equaling about a million vehicles some with fuel and some loaded with other combustible chemicals
- Over 150,000 commercial and private aircrafts plus thousands of warplanes from all countries with active militaries, all with fuel
- 90,000 or more armed battle tanks and over 100,000 additional military vehicles with fuel
- Billions of light and heavy construction and farm equipment with fuel
- Oil and natural gas from over 700 oil refineries and over 200,000 miles of oil pipelines full or partially filled.
- Billions of tanks of gasoline, propane gas, fuel oil, hydrogen, helium, oxygen and other explosive chemicals from across the planet
- Billions of commercial and military explosives plus several billions or trillions of rounds of ammunition

The violent reeling to and fro of the earth will shake into space all of the items mentioned above like a dog slinging water after a bath. The result will be the conversion of the landfills into gargantuan tsunamis of debris that will spread over millions of miles around the weakened and accelerating earth and its moon. The vast fields of debris will sweep through the solar system at astronomical speeds and create tremendous havoc in space. The speed of this explosive debris will be consistent with or greater than the speed of the earth.

> *Revelation 6:12-17 – And I beheld, when he had opened the sixth seal, lo there was a great earthquake, and the sun became black as sackcloth of hair, and the moon became like blood; and the stars of heaven fell unto the earth, even as a fig tree casteth her untimely figs, when she is shaken of a mighty wind. And the heaven departed as a scroll when it is rolled together; and every mountain and island were moved out of their places.*

Revelation describes the incredible speed of the earth, its moon and their tsunamis of debris as they travel around the sun. Scientists have estimated the distances between planets and the sun in millions of miles ranging from 29 million miles to 2.7 billion miles. In Revelation John indicates that great distances will be covered as quickly as someone can roll in a star-spangled scroll. Revelation also indicates that the earth will pass by stars so fast that the stars will appear to be figs falling from a tree in a mighty wind. The statement of stars falling to earth is another example of the writer speaking according to his level of scientific understanding. Our sun is a small star and is 865,000 miles in diameter and surely can't fall to the earth. John speaks of many stars falling to the earth which is an utter impossibility.

Currently the earth travels around the sun in a controlled orbit at 67,000 miles per hour. That speed is maintained today while it carries trillions of gallons of water. What will be the speed of a dissolved earth that is dissolved and without its water but is under a greatly increased influence of the sun due to its loss in weight? The earth and the molten moon will be like top-fuel celestial dragsters along a star-spangled course followed by tsunamis of debris also traveling at incredible speeds. Great distances will be covered in seconds. The earth and the moon will accelerate from the already established speed of 67.000 miles per hour as the sun's gravity slingshots them around it. They and their tsunamis of debris will not only be fiery dragsters but also fiery and massive projectiles capable of causing staggering devastation to whatever lies in their paths, including Mercury, Venus and Mars. Again, it is understood from Chapter 2 – Water Balanced that the loss of water on earth will jeopardize the stability and existence of the entire solar system.

Chapter 6 – The Heaven Is Ablaze!

We know that the universe consist of a great abundance of planets, stars, galaxies and numerous other celestial bodies and they are all engaged in a vast amount of celestial activities. How all of these are intertwined is not really known. Scientists do know that there have been extremely catastrophic events occurring in other galaxies, such as an exploding star or supernova, which had no noticeable effect upon our galaxy or our solar system. This book has continuously focused on the biblical writers' perceptions of what they saw in their visions and what they were inspired to write. Again, they had no advance knowledge of the universe as is available today so, when they speak of the heavens I assume they are referring to what is within their limited sight as well as their limited scientific knowledge. In this chapter there is a progression in the scriptures from the distress of the earth to the distress of the heavens.

> *2 Peter 3:10, 12 – But the day of the Lord will come as a thief in the night, in which the heavens shall pass away with a great noise... (12) Looking for and hasting unto the coming of the day of God, in which the heavens being on fire, shall be dissolved, and the elements shall melt with fervent heat?*

A review of 2 Peters 3:12 show that the writer at one point sees the heavens on fire. This is an expansion of the other scriptural references to the fire of the earth and the moon. Peter gives the same state of devastation to the heavens as is given to the earth. He writes that the heavens will be dissolved. I assume that the term "dissolved" means the same when referring to the earth and the heavens.

I believe the fiery and erratic flight patterns of the earth, the moon and the tsunamis of fiery and explosive debris will collide with one or more of the planets of our solar system. Earth is the third planet in a flat plane configuration of nine planets. Astronomers report that the planets are aligned on one plane almost like balls on a pool table or like race cars on a NASCAR speedway. They are also traveling at incredible speeds on that track. Mercury travels at 107,132 miles per hour, Venus at 78,364 miles per hour, Mars at 53,980 miles per hour and Earth at 67,000 miles per hour. Peter records a great noise in space and the heavens dissolved. It is understandable that there will be tremendous noise when the earth reels to and fro, quakes and slings the mountains like rams and produces great infernos on the surface. But Peter speaks of noise and fire in the heavens. Peter indicates that even though the planets are millions of miles apart, something involving the earth will be responsible for their fires and destruction which will contribute to the noise in space. He indicates that earth and the other planets will be destroyed in relatively the same time period. I believe what started on earth will be the cause of devastation throughout the solar system.

Scientists say there is no noise in space because the atoms and molecules that produce sound need matter or a medium upon which to act. Peter's record of a great noise in the heavens is evidence that there will be plenty of matter dispersed in the millions of miles between planets upon which the molecules can act to produce sound. The dissolving earth will produce massive trailing tsunamis of debris and there will be the sound of great rumblings as the planets come in contact with these tsunamis of debris and the core of the earth and the core of the moon. The trailing debris will consist of massive chunks from the mountains of Earth that will impact the surfaces of the planets with the power of nuclear weapons. The following reports of two meteor impacts give an idea of the amount of explosive energy that could be released upon impact with the planets by many of the items in the debris fields.

> Calculations show that a meteorite with a diameter of 30 m (229 ft), weighing about 300,000 tons, traveling at a velocity of 15 km/sec (33,500 miles/hour) would release energy equivalent to about 20 million tons of TNT.

(http://www.tulane.edu/~sanelson/Natural_Disasters/impacts.htm) (Meteorites/Velocity and Energy Release of Incoming Objects, December 1, 2014)

> (Jupiter) Astronomers estimated that the visible fragments of SL9 ranged in size from a few hundred metres to two kilometres across... This impact was estimated to have released an energy equivalent to

6,000,000 megatons of TNT (600 times
the world's nuclear arsenal).
(h t t p : / / e n . w i k i p e d i a . o r g / w i k i /
Comet_Shoemaker%E2%80%93Levy_9)
(Comet Shoemaker/Levy 9)

Impacts will come from not only the great boulders from
the fragmented mountains but also from the cars, planes,
trains, ships, military armaments, commercial hardware,
explosives and many of the other items previously listed
from the dissolved earth. They will devastate whatever lies
in their path with a barrage of successive impacts. Unlike
the meteor and the comet that impacted Jupiter, the fiery
and explosive debris from earth will arrive with more than
twice their speeds. Of course, the nuclear weapons in the
debris will impact as nuclear bombs but with explode with
much greater devastation due to their speed and depth of
penetration at impact.

If Earth, like a ball on a string, will have an altered
orbit and increased speed around the sun, so will the other
planets if collisions occur that reduce their masses and make
them also like lighter balls on a string. Their erratic and
accelerated flights will add tremendously to the chaos and
debris in space around the sun. There will be plenty of
material from explosions and collisions to produce plenty of
noise and fires to support Peter's vision of fire and noise in
the heavens. I can envision a medley of gargantuan Fourth
of July-like finales in space, ones that have gone horribly
wrong!

When discussing Peter's vision of a dissolving heaven,
we must consider all the significant celestial bodies that

will be affected by the earth, its moon, and the tsunamis of debris. Lying between Mars and Jupiter are more than 1.7 million asteroids that also revolve around the sun in what astronomers refer to as the Main Asteroid Belt.

> Over 200 asteroids are known to be larger than 100 km, and a survey in the infrared wavelengths has shown that the asteroid belt has 0.7–1.7 million asteroids with a diameter of 1 km or more.
> https://en.wikipedia.org/wiki/Asteroid_belt

Now the complete image of the chaos in space in the distance between the sun and Mars is the billions of boulders from every mountain, canyon and crust of the earth, billions of trees and plant life, billions of stone, wood and metallic frameworks from every residential and commercial buildings and other structures, billions of items from all the infrastructure, billions of private, commercial and military vehicles, billions of private, commercial and military explosive hardware, fragmentations from the interior planets and approximately two million asteroids from the Main Asteroid Belt. When the earth is smitten by the Spirit of God, the solar system will be like a dry mixture in a high speed blender which will be in contrast to creation where things were prepared by God in water.

Chapter 7 – The Attack on the Sun

While some of the tsunamis of debris cause havoc by setting the heaven ablaze, the solid cores of the earth and the moon and other debris will continue their trek for impacts on the sun. The sun will pull into itself two massive and ballistic balls of iron and explosive tsunamis of debris to which it will provide the necessary acceleration for maximum penetration. The sun will pull them as it has done to comets under its influence. The speed of a comet is increased as it approaches the sun.

> ...the Moon has an iron rich core with the radius of 330 ± 20 km (410 miles diameter)... the solid inner core made of pure iron...
> (http://en.wikipedia.org/wiki/ Internal_structure_of_the_Moon.)

> Composed mainly of iron, Earth's core consists of a solid inner core about 2,400 kilometers in diameter (1491 miles)...
> (http://www.sciencedaily.com/ releases/2008/03/080310131507.htm)
> (Science Daily, March 10, 2008)

What will be the impact of these iron balls upon the sun and the sun's impact upon them? Will the approaching chaos of the earth, the moon and the fiery tsunamis of debris survive the sun's torrid atmosphere? Astronomers constantly observe and report on the impacts of comets on the sun. Their report gives us an idea of the impact:

> The comet seen by Raftery and her fellow researchers apparently survived the intense heat of the sun's outer atmosphere… and disappeared in the chromospheres; … not only surviving the extreme temperatures but the strong solar winds as well, before finally evaporating.
> (http://www.space.com/scienceastronomy/comet-collision-with-sun-aas216-100524.html) (Space.com, May 24, 2010)

The report states that the head of a comet survived the entry into the sun's atmosphere and was evaporated after traveling deep inside the second layer. The partially vaporized head of a comet is very miniscule compared to the earth and the moon's iron cores and the tsunamis of destructive debris that will arrive. If the metallic portion of a comet survived then the billions of items in the explosive debris will surely penetrate deep inside the sun along with the iron cores of the earth and the moon. The sun will be impacted with brutal force! The resulting affect will be a supernova which is the explosion of the sun and eventually a dead star as prophesized by Revelation 6:12.

Revelation 6:12 – And I beheld, when he had opened the sixth seal, lo there was a great earthquake, and the sun became black as sackcloth of hair, and the moon became like blood; ...

In order for John to see our sun black as sackcloth of hair the continuous explosions of hydrogen and helium in the sun must cease and that cessation must results in a black star or a dead star.

The sun is approximately 865,000 miles in diameter. An impact with the earth's core which has a diameter of 1,491 miles would be considered an insignificant event by some scientists in terms of how it would affect the sun. Even though the sun is 865,000 miles in diameter, the onslaught of billions of projectiles that are traveling at speeds greatly exceeding 67,000 miles per hour will mean death by a billion cuts. I believe the onslaught will indeed contribute to the destruction of the sun. (See drawing "Attack on the Sun") The book of Revelation records the sun will be "black as sackcloth of hair". I believe that when John speaks of hair he is actually seeing the streaks of billions of objects that will arrive to the sun. The heat of the sun will set them on fire which will produce dark streaks of smoke as they impact the sun. These streaks appeared to John as hair because he is speaking as a common man of ancient time who was not given advance knowledge of astronomy.

The prophet Enoch went to heaven and was allowed to return to earth and write about his experience. He recorded in the Book of the Secrets of the Prophet Enoch, Chapter

34 that God spoke to him concerning the destruction of the earth.

> *The Book of the Secrets of Enoch Chapter 34 –*
> *And therefore I will bring down a great deluge*
> *upon the earth and will destroy all men, and*
> *the whole earth will crumble together into*
> *great darkness.*

According to Enoch, the final destination for the physical earth is a place of great darkness. I believe that place is the same darkness John saw in Revelation 6:12 which is the black remnant of the sun.

I have outlined the destruction of the earth and the moon and the expansion of the chaos to the adjacent planets of Mars, Venus and Mercury and to the asteroid belt. But there is more to our solar system that must be accounted for as also part of this terrible time. Earth thrives in a solar system with gas giants as they are called in the field of astronomy. Uranus, Jupiter, Neptune and Saturn have atmospheres that are composed of lethal combinations of highly explosive gases: hydrogen, helium and methane.

- Uranus – 85% Hydrogen, 12% Helium, 3% Methane
- Jupiter – 86% Hydrogen, 13% Helium, 1% Methane
- Neptune – 85% Hydrogen, 13% Helium, 2% Methane
- Saturn – 94% Hydrogen, 6% Helium
  (http://en.wikipedia.org/wiki/Methane)

I noticed that our solar system has a very curious planetary configuration. There are four planets close to the sun that have solid masses and iron cores, and they are surrounded by the asteroid belt followed by four planets that are primarily gas balls. Was our solar system created with a self-destruct feature that will be activated by the removal of water? We can possibly add these gas balls to the celestial chaos of destruction which will consist of the fiery duo of the earth and the moon, the fiery tsunamis of debris from earth, the fragmentations and possibly the iron cores from Venus, Mercury and Mars, plus the two million asteroids from the Main Asteroid Belt. All of these will be subject to the great gravitational pull of the sun. The fuel determines the fire and the heaven will be full of fuel for continuous explosions and the demise of the sun.

There is a question as to whether the great explosions will affect the total galaxy or just our solar system. I am unable to develop an opinion from the scriptures whether John and others saw in their visions the destruction of the entire universe, the galaxy, or just our solar system. It doesn't seem logical that the billions of stars in the universe will suffer the fate of our solar system when the reason for the destruction of the heaven and the earth will be the sins of men on earth. Since our solar system is one among billions upon billions of stars and planets in the universe, it seems unnecessary to destroy the entire universe to simply create another minute set of celestial bodies referred to in the Bible as the new heaven and the new earth. But, I wonder if the new heaven and earth that John saw are new selections from among the billions of celestial bodies that are currently in the universe. I wonder this because for the first heaven and earth there is the story of creation with water as the deep, the gathering together of water and the appearance of he dry land. But, for the new heaven and earth there are no creation events recorded. There is only the appearance of a new heaven and earth. There is no second Big Bang. John sees an already existing and different heaven and earth – an earth without water that will not have a sun which means it will not revolve around a star.

> *Revelation 22:5 – And there shall be no night*
> *there; and they need no lamp neither light of*
> *the sun; for the Lord God giveth them light,*
> *and they shall reign forever and ever.*

The scriptures record an earth on fire, a moon on fire, a heaven on fire and a black sun but do not explain what will happen to the sun afterward. We do know that many dead stars or black holes currently exist in the universe.

The Attack on the Sun

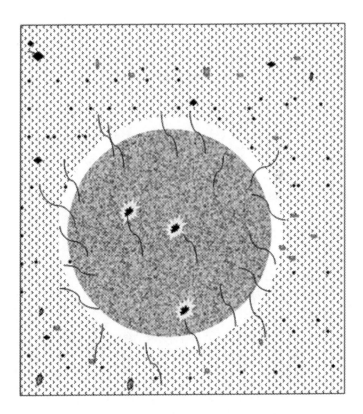

The Sun became "black as sackcloth of hair"

The space around the sun will be filled with billions of items from the tsunamis of debris from Earth, the other planets and the asteroid belt. These items will enter the sun's atmosphere at speeds greater than 67,000 mph and will be set aflame prior to impact which will produce the black streaks that appear to be hair.

Chapter 8 – Water and the Spirits

I have discussed so far three facts about water: God called out water as the deep at the beginning of Creation; John records in Revelation that water will flow from the throne of God and; the prophet Enoch wrote that he saw a quantity of water in heaven that was greater than the waters on earth. It appears that water straddles the natural and spiritual world. With that thought in mind I was curious about the relationship of water with spirits from heaven and spirits that will go to heaven.

> *Luke 8:31- 32 – And they besought him that he would not command them to go out into the deep. And there was there an herd of many swine, feeding on the mountain, and they besought him that he would allow them to enter into them. And he permitted them.*

> *Mark 5:10 – And he besought him much that he would not send them away out of the country.*

The gospel of Luke records that Jesus met a deranged man who was possessed with many demons who called themselves collectively as Legion. The demons strongly besought Jesus for permission to enter swine and wanted not to be sent to the deep. It is curious that the demons referred to the waters as the deep which is the same term used for water in the book of Genesis during Creation. The demons seem to indicate that the water of the deep offered an unpleasant situation which could have been termination, confinement or perhaps torture. Their choices were: to the deep, to the swine, to the air, or to other men which Jesus, of course, would not have allowed. Two of the choices involved water as the deep and the atmosphere which came from the deep. If the water and the air were not desirable options then God created a hostile environment for the demons when he created the earth with three-fourth water and a watery atmosphere. It seems logical to assume that if there was a war in heaven and Satan and his followers were expel to Earth, the expulsion was not for the purpose of vacationing but confinement. Also, taking another look at Creation, we can theorize that the emergence of dry land offered some form of respite or freedom for the demons in a water prison.

The demons statements raise other questions such as why were the swine and men more desirable than the water and the air. How could natural water affect the status of spirits? Why was it imperative for them to have a living host in which to dwell? It seems that the physical nature of the earth, which is dominated top to bottom by water, is not a habitat of pleasure for demons. God created the heaven and the earth and something that was created offered the solution to the intent of banishment and no return to heaven. I believe that the massive amount of water on this earth is an element of confinement and, animals and mankind offer demonic spirits their very limited freedom of operation for an undisclosed length of time. We know the story of Adam and Eve and the statement in Genesis 3:1 that the serpent was more subtle than any beast of the field and he tempted Eve.

The following scripture from the corresponding book of Matthew shows that the same demons looked at Jesus and was concerned about torment and the only thing that Jesus presented was himself which was the embodiment of the Spirit of God.

> *Matthew 8:29 – And, behold, they cried out, saying, What have we to do with thee, Jesus, thou son of God? Art thou come here to torment us before the time?*

At one point the demons were distressed about two things: Jesus (the Spirit and fire) and the deep (water). Unfortunately for them, when they entered the herd of swine, the herd of two thousand swine ran down the hill to the sea and drowned themselves. Why? Why did two thousand swine make a collective decision to run down the hill in a frantic effort to seek water for the purpose of suicide? I can imagine the scene of a few hundred swine drowning at the water's edge and others climbing across their bodies to get to the water to also drown themselves. There were two thousand swine splashing and convulsing in the water until death. The death of the swine raises the question as to what happened to the demonic spirits that possessed them, the ones that were afraid of the deep.

As was stated previously, water straddles the natural and the spiritual world. Revelation 20:13-14 states that the sea will retain spirits of the dead that will be released on the Day of Judgment.

> *Revelation 20:13-14 – And the sea gave up the dead that were in it, and death and hades (hell) delivered up the dead that were in them; and they were judged every man according to their works. (14) And death and hades (hell) were cast into the lake of fire. This is the second death.*

The above reference is an indication that water continues after the end of the world. The scriptures name three locations for the dead at the end time: sea, death and hades (hell). After the heaven and the earth pass away the only evidence of mankind will be the souls of men in the three locations. Two of the three (death and Hades) will be cast into the lake of fire. What will happen to the sea (water)? Water will be retained by God because it is one of his divine tools. Death and hell will no longer be needed since there will be no more death or unrighteousness after the heaven and the earth pass away. If we place the water in Genesis beside the water in Revelation we can see water as key to the origin of life and water as a harbor for souls after life. From this we can understand that water transcends life and death. If water will have souls to give up then we can understand why water was given its own distinct designation as Sea at creation. We can understand why the demons besought Jesus not to send them to the deep. It appears that water would have restricted or confined them in some manner.

If we continue with the concept that water is a part of both the natural world and the spiritual world, we can look closer at one of Jesus' teachings that involved water. There is a familiar parable in the Bible where Jesus makes reference to the status of a man's soul in hell. The parable is commonly discussed in terms of hell's fire but I believe it is more of an emphasis on a lack of water and a great thirst for water.

> *Luke 16:24 – And he cried and said, Father Abraham, have mercy on me, and send Lazarus, that he may dip the tip of his finger in water, and cool my tongue, for I am tormented in this flame.*

We know that water is an extinguisher of fire because in the natural world we have had many occasions where that has happened. But, in Revelation God will destroy hell not by casting it into water but into fire. It seems a great fire will be cast into a greater fire. It is a common belief that hell is a place of much fire and I have heard many references to the fire in hell such as "It's going to be hotter than that in hell" and many others. All of the statements highlight the temperature of a fire in hell. The above scripture is an excerpt from one of Jesus' parables that teaches about a rich man who mistreated a poor man and the rich man is tormented in hell after death. This parable should be a sure example of torment by fire in hell. The people who made the hell comments and equated hell's fire with natural fire were very familiar with the pain and suffering caused by a severe burn. Is it conceivable that anyone could engage in a conversation with another person at a distance while burning in natural flames? The common sight of extreme burns is hysterical flight and screams. Many cinematic portrayals of hell show people with melting red faces who are screaming to the top of their voices in the midst of many natural flames. But, the conversations in the parable seem to indicate that it is the lack of water that presents the torment. The rich man wanted water to soothe the inside via his tongue. The rich man states that he is in "this flame" which indicates one flame. It is the same flame or fire that removed water from Lot's wife, from the sons of Aaron, from Sodom and Gomorrah, from the Red Sea and the Jordan River, and will remove water from the combatants against God in the end time. It is the fire of the Spirit of God, the executor of God's will. It is the same fire that Jesus embodied in the presence of the demons when they questioned him about the prospect of being tormented.

Why did Jesus give a reference to water in a parable about hell and where was the water located? Even though the story is a parable, I am confident that Jesus used factual information in his teachings. Jesus acknowledged the presence of water. The parable seems to indicate that there was torment in the flame for the ungodly and water across the gulf for those not being tormented. That concept conforms to Revelation 20:13-14 where it says that the sea will give up the dead that is in it and death and hell will give up the dead that are in them. Jesus acknowledged the presence of the sea and hell with death appearing to be the distributor of souls into either location.

The request for water by the rich man shows that he and the others in hell have a thirst that is not quenched. No amount of water would be able to satisfy their thirst because the fire they are in is an unquenchable fire that controls water, not by its temperature, but by its inherent nature as the Spirit of God. Those who prefer the idea of natural flames burning an individual in hell must understand that being in a never ending desert without a drop of water is also great torment. I asked myself what is the need for flames as in a natural fire and how much heat God would have to produce in hell to torment billions of souls. I often sight the power of a hydrogen bomb perched on someone head and detonated – the body is vaporized but the soul survives for judgment. I am then reminded that God works not by power or might but by his Spirit. God's way is as simple as a molecule of water. Why create a great fire that will evaporate water when the simple removal of water will suffice? Why cause volcanoes and earthquakes or a fire to destroy Sodom and Gomorrah, Lot's wife and the sons of Aaron when the removal of water was simpler and brought devastation to a selected group of people? Why would ashes be more preferable than pillars of salt? In hell, what would be the sadistic purpose of flames when the Spirit of God can achieve the same result which is a great thirst for water? The two contrasting pictures of judgment are souls from death and hell with unquenched thirst who are destined for the lake of fire and souls from the water many of whom are destined for the new earth to drink crystal clear water from living fountains of God.

> *Revelation 7:17 – For the Lamb who is in the midst of the throne shall feed them, and shall lead them unto living fountains of waters; and shall wipe away all tears from their eyes.*

There is a recurring theme in the Bible with water in the forefront: nature coming out of water during creation; believers emerging out of water during baptism; souls coming out of water on the Day of Judgment.

Chapter 9 – Conclusion

To consider the incredibly catastrophic events that will mark the destruction of the earth, moon, sun and the solar system is a complex and challenging task. It is also challenging to understand how the Spirit of God manipulated and will manipulate the simple molecules of water to accomplish deeds for and against mankind. Why water is such a special creation will not be known until it is revealed at the end. This book presents the idea that God used water as the carrier for the chemistry of the universe when he prepared it as the deep. The book of Genesis records that four of the six days of creation was dominated by actions to or actions occurring out of water – Genesis 1:2, 1:6-8, 1:9-10, 1:20-23. After the creation of mankind water was designated as one of the divine witnesses on earth.

> *1 John 5:7-8 – For there are three that bear record in heaven, the Father, the Word, and the Holy Spirit; and these three are one. And there are three that bear witness in earth, the Spirit, and the water, and the blood; and these three agree in one.*

As a witness and a divine tool of God, water has a key role in the biblical history of man. Water was the center of attention at the Red Sea, and had a major role at Mt. Carmel and in Sodom and Gomorrah. Its spiritual clout will be more evident when it changes its role on the day of the Lord when the heaven and the earth pass away.

There is a familiar scripture that helps shed light on the removal of water as the catalyst to destruction on the day of the Lord:

> *2 Peter 3:10 – But the day of the Lord will come as a thief in the night…*

The swift action of the Spirit to remove water is more God-like than a cinematic apocalyptic war between good and evil involving machines and weapons that are predicted to destroy the earth. War does not explain a clean dissolved earth and a dissolved heaven, a sun black as sackcloth of hair and a moon like blood. The prophet Zechariah states that there is a definite difference in the workings of the Spirit of God and the interactions within the natural world. Natural power and might are shown in volcanoes, earthquakes, natural fires and war. The Spirit of God simply and quietly pulls the pin and allows life and the solar system to unravel and crumble and the pin is water.

> *Zechariah 4:6 – Then he answered and spoke unto me, saying, Not by might, nor by power, but by my Spirit, saith the Lord of hosts.*

I think of God's actions in Sodom and Gomorrah and at the end time and the reference to "a thief in the night, as spiritual special ops. The angels rescued Lot's family and used only the necessary force against the inhabitants of the city to seal the rescue. After the family was delivered, the silent blast of the Spirit of God like a thief in the night removed the water which destroyed the cities. At the end time Jesus will rescue his people from the earth during the theological rapture and, at an appointed time, a silent blast of spiritual fire will again remove water like a thief in the night which will lead to the destruction of earth and its inhabitants. The tales of Armageddon and hell's fire, volcanoes and earthquakes make men expect the end to be initiated by an aerial bombardment, the rumbling of the ground, drum beats and immediate visuals of the coming destruction. Lot heard and saw nothing but his wife as a pillar of salt. Sodom and Gomorrah were destroyed in an instant while Abraham slept and no one was able to escape. The sons of Aaron were destroyed but their clothes were not scattered. There will be no sign but the swiftness of fire and brimstone and the stealthy removal of water.

The end of the heaven and the earth will not signify water's final performance. Water will make a re-appearance on the new earth even though the new earth will be prepared without the sea.

> *Revelation 21:1 – And I saw a new heaven and a new earth; for the first heaven and the first earth were passed away, and there was no more sea.*

"There was no more sea" means that the new heaven and the new earth will not be a result of the manipulation of water, such as the compression of the deep that I believe occurred for the first heaven and earth. There will not be a deep so there will be no new creation activities such as those recorded in Genesis. The water on the new earth will be crystal clear and will be without the abundant elements that were in the deep.

The book of Genesis states that in the beginning God created the heaven and the earth and elaborated on what God did during the six days of creation. In Revelation John sees a new heaven and a new earth that is already formed. Other writers wrote about the demise of the old heaven and earth but none speak of what God will do to bring about the new worlds with a waterless earth. But the scriptures do explain that there will be water provided in a different manner. God will add water as needed.

> *Revelation 22:1 – And he showeth me a pure river of water of life, clear as crystal, proceeding out of the throne of God and of the Lamb.*

God has demonstrated throughout the Bible that he is not only a God of fire but also a God of water. God, the artist, has two major materials that he uses throughout his vision and they are fire (Spirit) and water, and he began and ended his project of creation with both. Many people focus primarily upon fire in their Bible studies because they often equate spiritual fire with natural fire and natural fire implies action, power and destruction. Power and destruction are believed to best represent the power of God. But a closer look at water reveals that it is also a creditable representative of God and it resides at his throne.

In Revelation 7:17 the writer records that God will feed his people but there is only a brief statement of the nature of the food but emphasis is definitely given to the nature of the drink which is crystal clear water. This book mentions three locations for water between now and eternity which I believe makes it possibly the most utilized molecule of all times. Those three locations are:

1. The waters of earth
2. The water in heaven as seen by the prophet Enoch:

   The Book of the Secrets of the Prophet Enoch Chapter 3 - … and they placed me on the first heaven and showed me a very great Sea, greater than the earthly sea.

3. The water on the new earth from the throne of God

Seeing then that water will always have a special place with God, it should also have a special place with us. A cool drink of water is very refreshing and it is also divine.

Bibliography

BiblePlaces.com, http://www.bibleplaces.com/deadsea.htm

Britannica.com,http://www.britannica.com/EBchecked/
topic/531121/seawater/301665/Salinity-Distribution

Explainthatstuff.com, http://www.explainthatstuff.com/
glass.html

Extreme Science, http://www.extremescience.com/zoom/
index.php/earth-records/37-dead-sea

Extreme Science, http://www.extremescience.com/zoom/
index.php/space/35-space-science/77-about-the-moon

Geology for Kids, http://www.kidsgeo.com/geology-for-
kids/0052-volcanoes-and-plant-life.php

Hydrogen Cars Now, http://www.hydrogencarsnow.com/
hydrogen-from-water.htm

NASA Science, http://science.nasa.gov/astrophysics/
focus-areas/black-holes/

National Aeronautical and Space Administration, http://imagine.gsfc.nasa.gov/docs/ask_astro/answers/970401c.html

Nine Planets.org, http://www.nineplanets.org/sol.html, January 25, 2009

Northwestern.edu. http://www.qrg.northwestern.edu/projects/vss/docs/space-environment/1-what-is-a-comet.html

Science Daily, http://www.sciencedaily.com/releases/2008/03/080310131507.htm

Science Daily, http://www.sciencedaily.com/releases/2008/03/080310131507.htm

Space.com

Space.com, http://www.space.com/6564-edge-space.html

Space.com., http://www.space.com/scienceastronomy/comet-collision-with-sun-aas216-100524.html

Space.com, http://www.space.com/scienceastronomy/060821_mystery_monday.html

The Scofield Study Bible, 1976 Edition, Authorized King James Version, Oxford Press, Inc.

Tulane University, http://www.tulane.edu/~sanelson/Natural_Disasters/impacts.htm

UMD Right Now, http://www.newsdesk.umd.edu/scitech/ release.cfm?ArticleID=1213ds

US Geological Survey, http://ga.water.usgs.gov/edu/ waterproperties.html

Wikipedia, http://en.wikipedia.org/wiki/Water_cycle

Wikipedia.com, http://en.wikipedia.org/wiki/Methane

Wikipedia, http://en.wikipedia.org/wiki/Comet_Shoemaker %E2%80%93Levy_9

Wikipedia, http://en.wikipedia.org/wiki/Internal_structure _of_the_Moon.)

Wikipedia.com, http://en.wikipedia.org/wiki/Deuterium

\Woods Hole Oceanographic Institution, Deeply Submerged Volcanoes Blow Their Tops, www.whoi.edu/oceanus/ viewArticle

Printed in the United States
By Bookmasters